ANIMALS & ME

Horses and Me

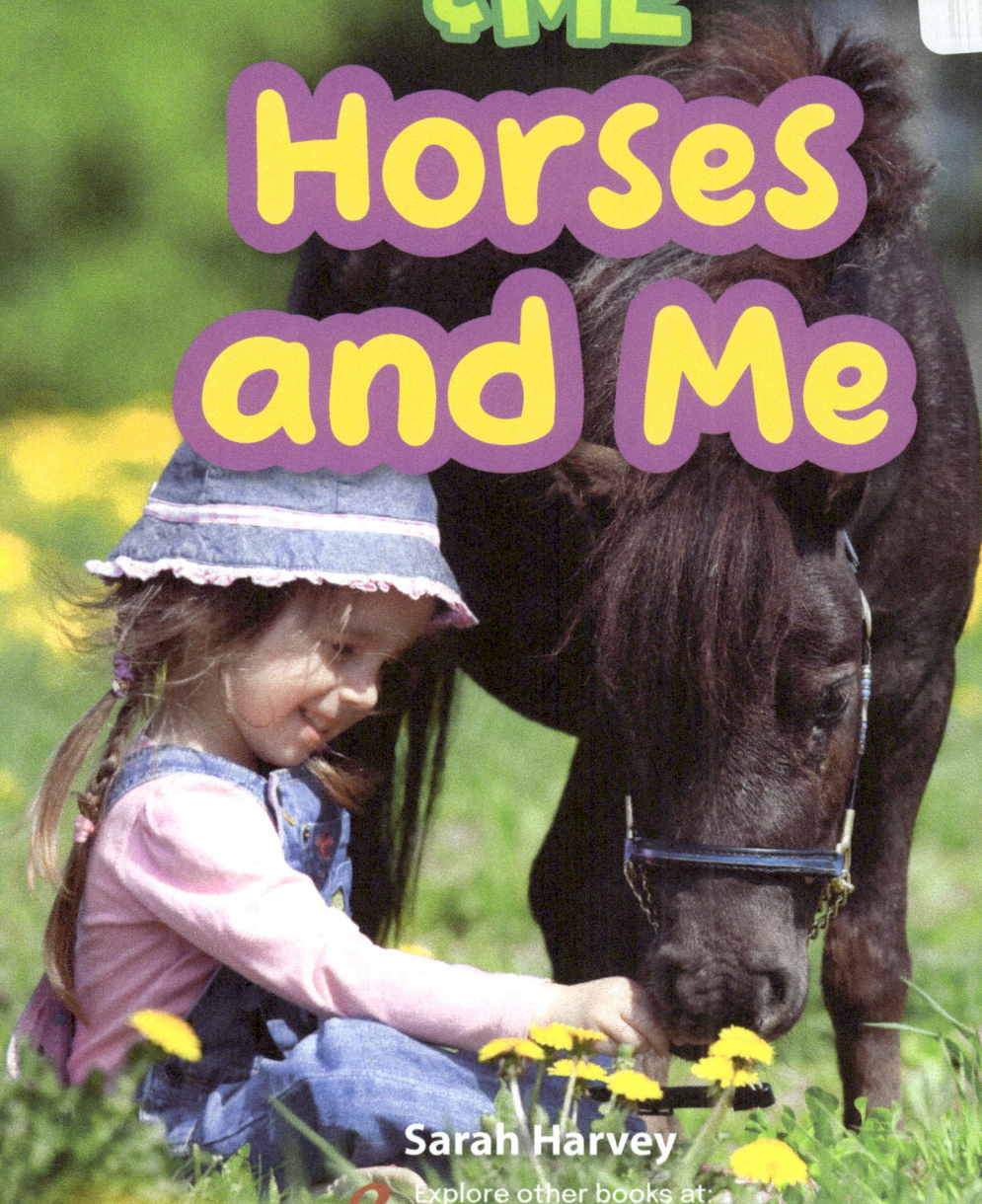

Sarah Harvey

Explore other books at:
WWW.ENGAGEBOOKS.COM

VANCOUVER, B.C.

WWW.ENGAGEBOOKS.COM

Horses and Me
Animals and Me
Harvey, Sarah N., 1950 –
Edited by: A.R. Roumanis
Text © 2022 Engage Books
Design © 2022 Engage Books

Text set in GelPenUpright

FIRST EDITION / FIRST PRINTING

LIBRARY AND ARCHIVES CANADA CATALOGUING IN PUBLICATION

Title: Horses and me / by Sarah Harvey.
Names: Harvey, Sarah N., 1950- author.
Description: Series statement: Animals and me

Identifiers: Canadiana (print) 2022039542X | Canadiana (ebook) 20220395438
ISBN 978-1-77476-692-7 (hardcover)
ISBN 978-1-77476-693-4 (softcover)
ISBN 978-1-77476-694-1 (epub)
ISBN 978-1-77476-695-8 (pdf)

Subjects:
LCSH: Horses—Juvenile literature.
LCSH: Horses—Behavior—Juvenile literature.
LCSH: Human behavior—Juvenile literature.

Classification: LCC SF302 .H37 2022 | DDC J636.1—DC23

This project has been made possible in part by the Government of Canada.

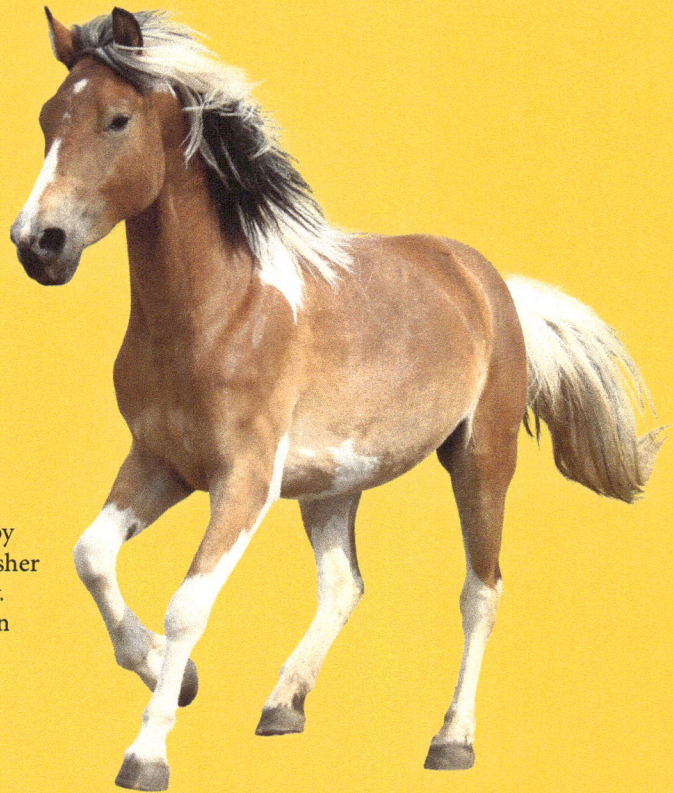

Canada

What do you know
about horses?

3

Horses live all over the world, except where it's very cold.

4

Do you like the cold?

5

Horses are related to zebras and donkeys.

Who are you related to?

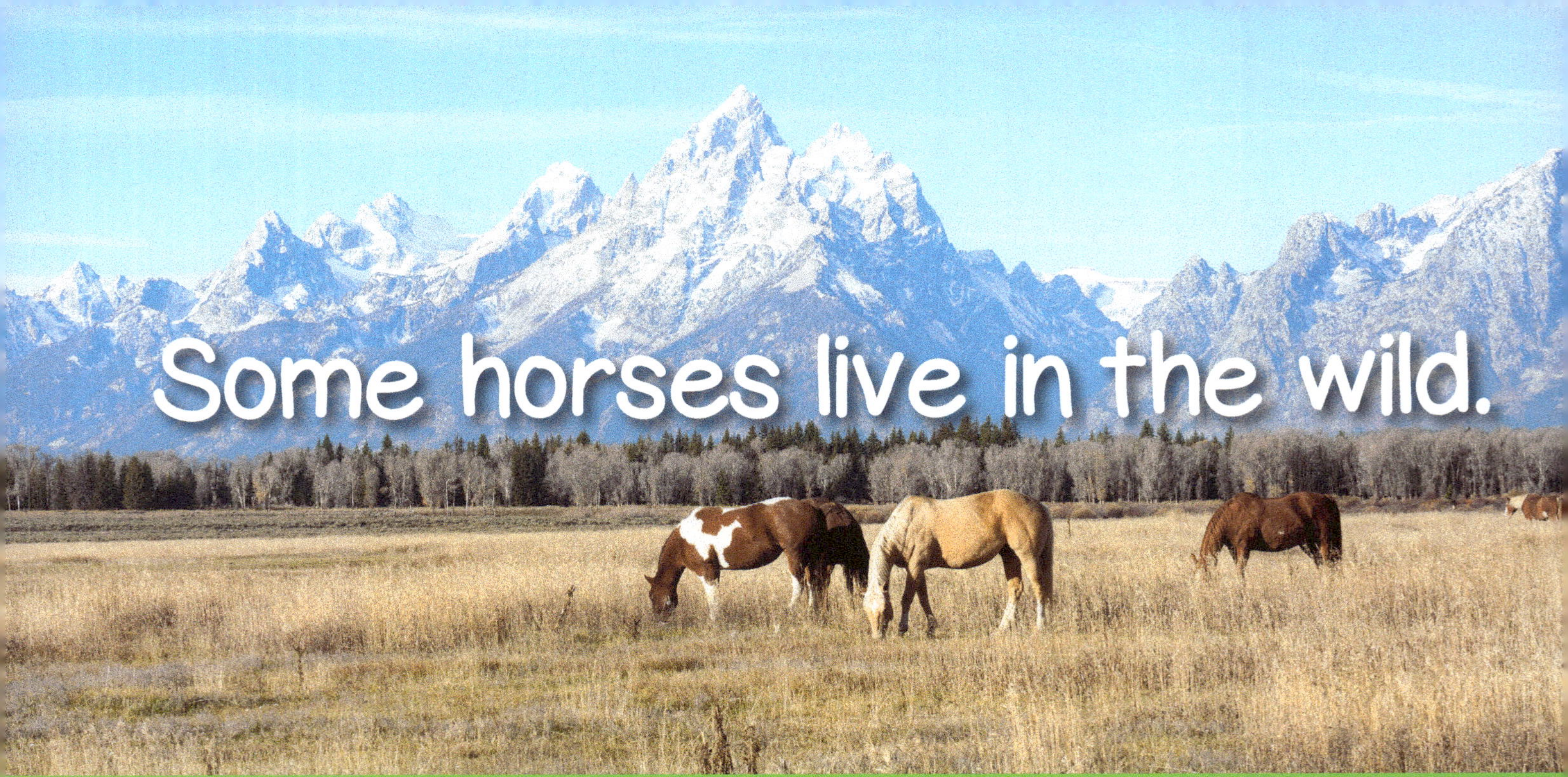

Some horses live in the wild.

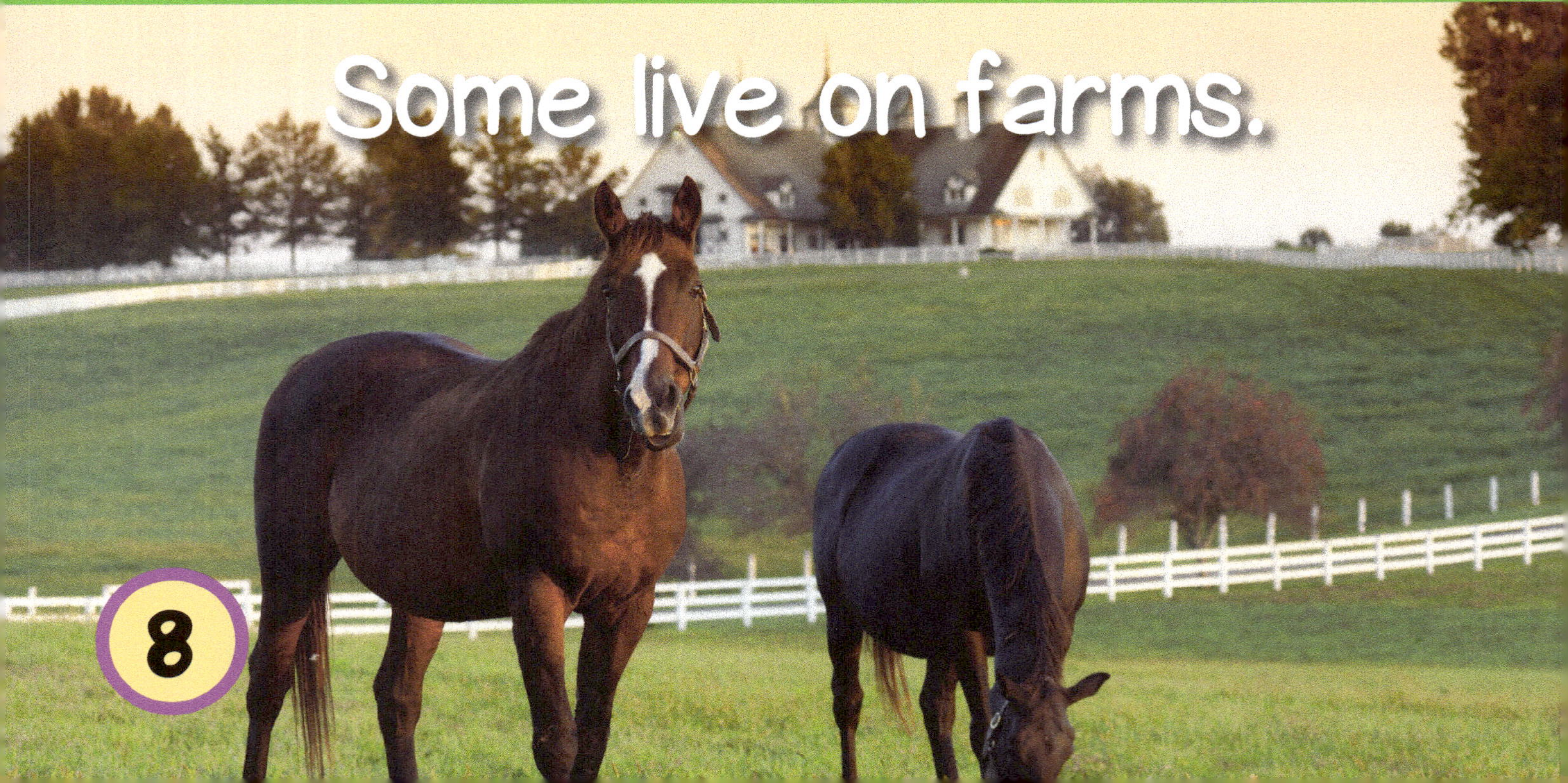

Some live on farms.

What other animals live on farms?

Ponies are the
smallest horses.

They are very gentle.

Would you like to ride a pony?

A baby horse is called a foal.

When it's a bit older, it's called a colt or a filly.

Are you a colt or a filly?

Horses eat grass and hay for up to 17 hours a day.

How many hours a day
do you eat?

15

Horses have long hair on their necks called a mane.

How long is your mane?

17

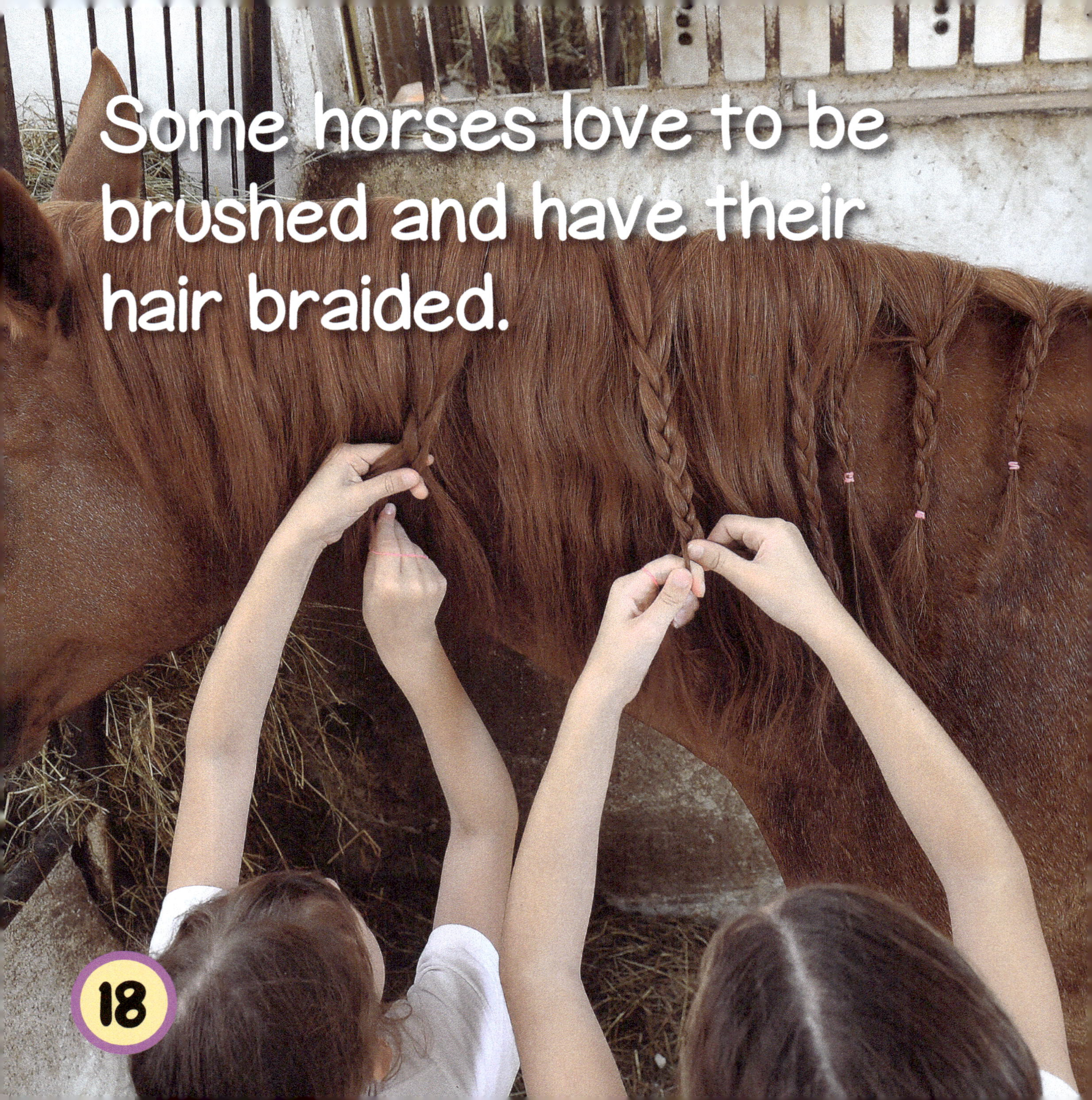

Some horses love to be brushed and have their hair braided.

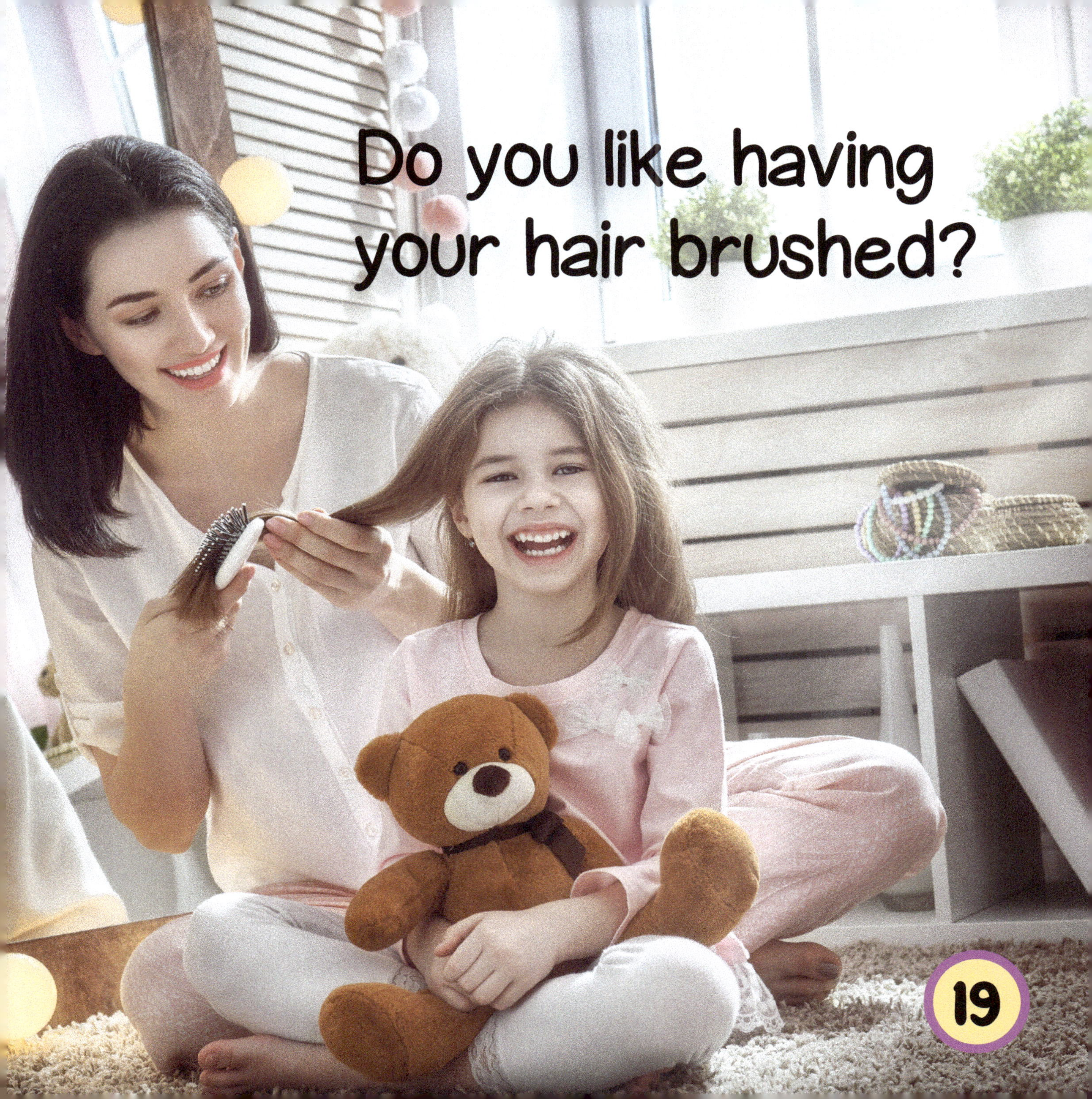

Do you like having your hair brushed?

Horses can talk with their ears. If a horse's ears are forward, it might be curious.

What are you curious about?

Wild horses can get lonely if they aren't with their herd.

Do you ever feel lonely?

23

There are five shapes of teeth in a horse's mouth.

How many shapes of teeth do you have?

25

Some horses need horseshoes to protect their hooves.

Tap dance shoes have
metal on the bottom.

Racehorses run very fast.

How fast can you run?

Some horses are trained to jump.

Where do you like to jump?

31

www.ingramcontent.com/pod-product-compliance
Lightning Source LLC
Chambersburg PA
CBHW041435040426
42452CB00023B/2983